BOOK TWO

NOTESPELLER
STORIES & GAMES

TRAVEL THROUGH TIME

KAREN HARRINGTON

Ancient   Renaissance   Classical   Contemporary

Medieval   Baroque   Romantic

ISBN 978-1-4584-1785-5

HAL•LEONARD®
CORPORATION

7777 W. BLUEMOUND RD. P.O. BOX 13819 MILWAUKEE, WI 53213

In Australia Contact:
Hal Leonard Australia Pty. Ltd.
4 Lentara Court
Cheltenham, Victoria, 3192 Australia
Email: ausadmin@halleonard.com.au

Visit Hal Leonard Online at
www.halleonard.com

NOTES FOUND IN THE STORIES AND GAMES

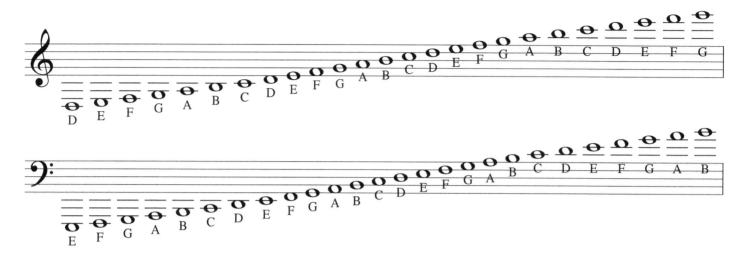

A Message to Teachers: **The Notespeller Stories and Games Book 2** naturally follows book 1 and presents note recognition activities that coordinate with any method. Book 2 uses interesting historical facts to provide students an enjoyable way of increasing their note reading skills. The stories teach notes on the staff, ledger line notes, and notes within key signatures, and uses different note values. The stories also include enharmonic and interval activities.

Students will enjoy creating words and stories from the musical alphabet while getting a sense of what it might have been like to live in different centuries.

I hope you and your students enjoy the book.

A Message to Students: As you progress through this notespeller, I hope you will learn not only the notes on the staff, but also some interesting facts about the way people have lived through the centuries. I have had a good time creating stories for you to complete and puzzles for you to solve. Have a good time, and make learning and music important parts of your life.

–Karen Harrington

ACKNOWLEDGEMENTS: Thanks to my editor Jennifer Linn, for her ideas, expertise, and encouragement. Thanks also to my friend and colleague Philelle McBrayer and my husband, John, for their ideas.

ABOUT THE AUTHOR: Karen Harrington, NCTM, maintains a private studio in Tulsa, Oklahoma, where she has taught piano for over thirty years. A graduate of the University of Oklahoma, she holds a BME degree with piano emphasis. Before opening her independent studio, Karen taught music in the Tulsa Public Schools for eight years. She has also taught at the University of Tulsa.

Karen served for two years on the board of directors of the Music Teachers National Association, as president of Tulsa Accredited Music Teachers Association, and as Northeast District President and Vice President of Oklahoma Music Teachers Association. Karen is currently President-elect of OMTA. She is a member of Tulsa Piano Study Club and serves as a clinician and adjudicator for her state and local associations.

In addition to creating the **Notespeller Stories books 1 and 2**, Karen is also co-author of the **Hal Leonard Student Piano Library Piano Theory Workbooks**, author of the method's three **Notespellers**, as well as two reproducible books titled, **Tic-Tac-Toe Music Games** and **Piano Teacher's Resource Kit**.

CONTENTS

TREBLE AND BASS LINE AND SPACE NOTES

Imagine Living in Another Time

In the gray boxes write the names of the notes.

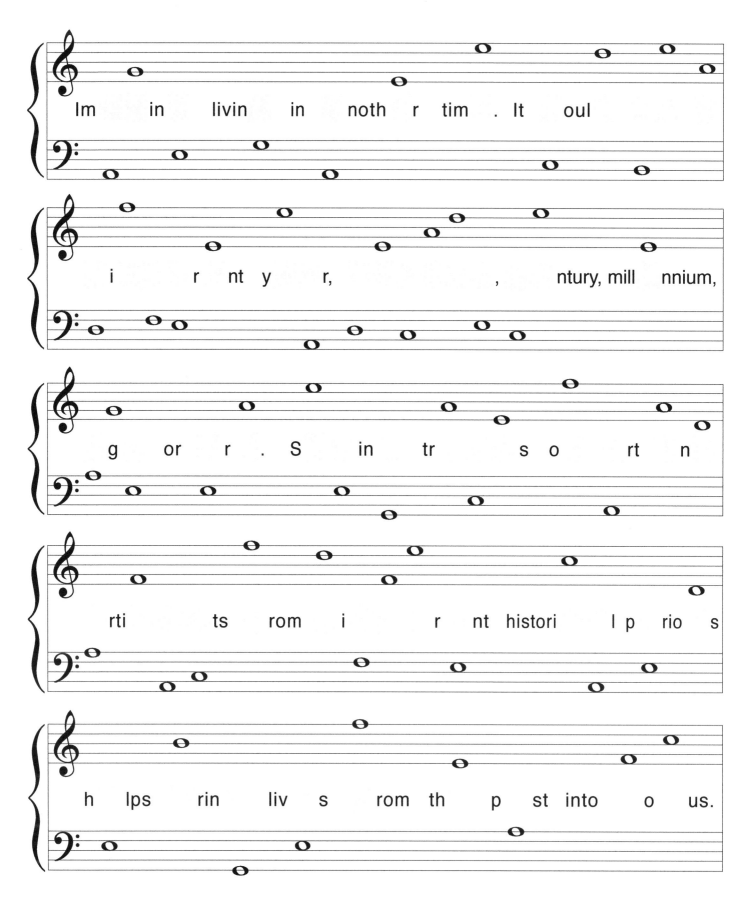

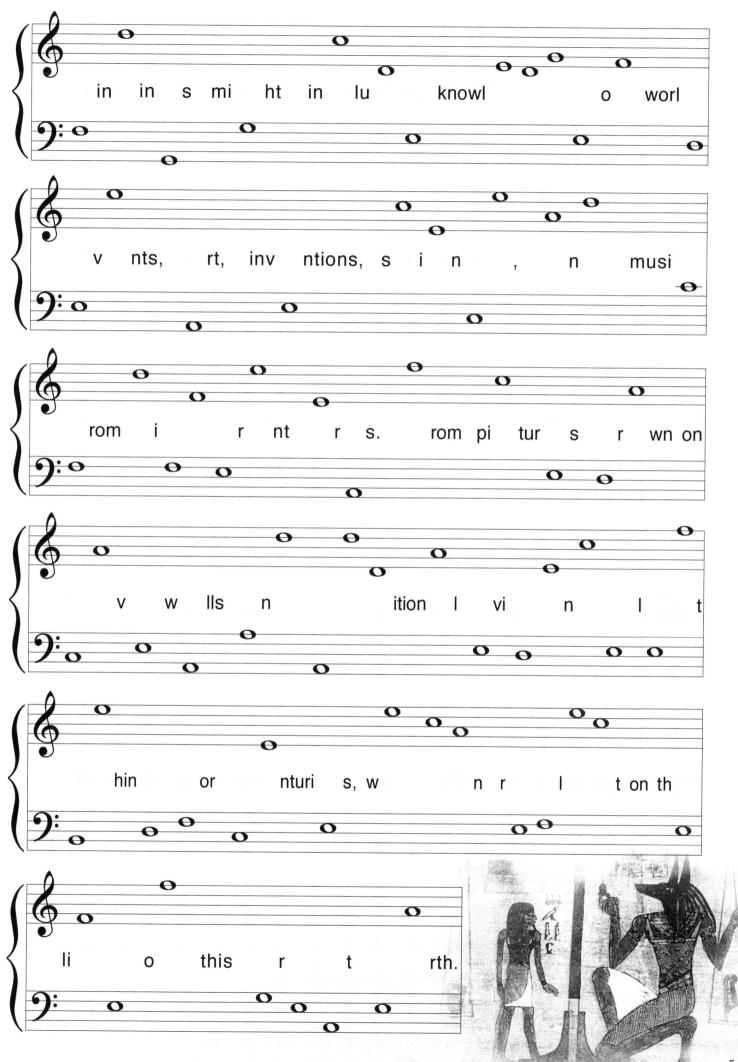

5

SHARPS, FLATS AND NATURALS
The Beginning of Music

Name the notes in the gray boxes. On the staff draw a sharp before each "F," a flat before each "D" and a natural before each "E."

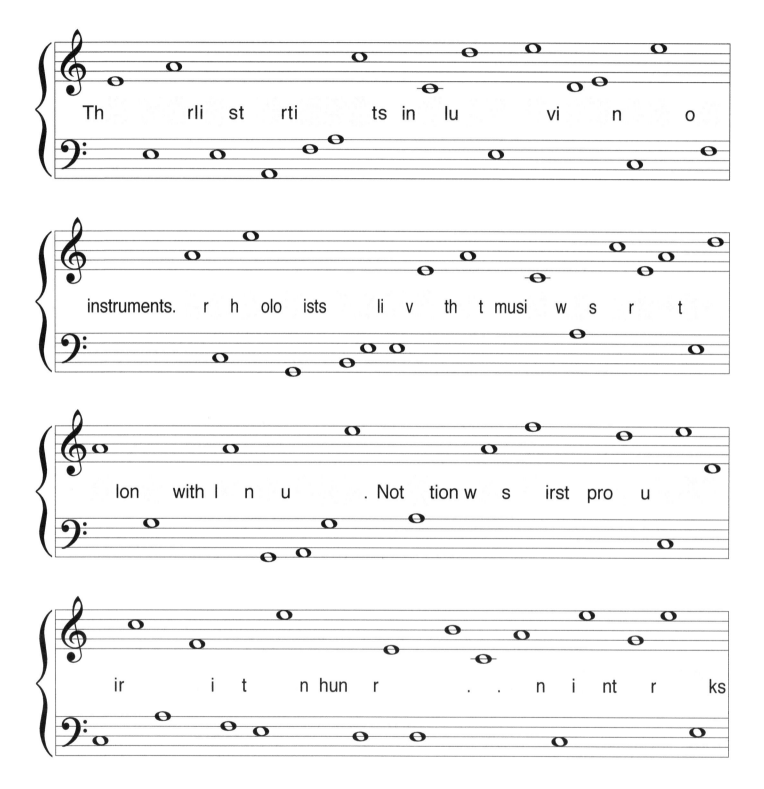

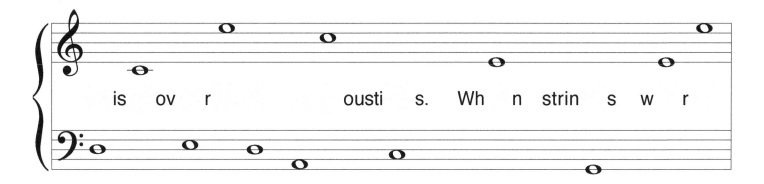

is ov r ousti s. Wh n strin s w r

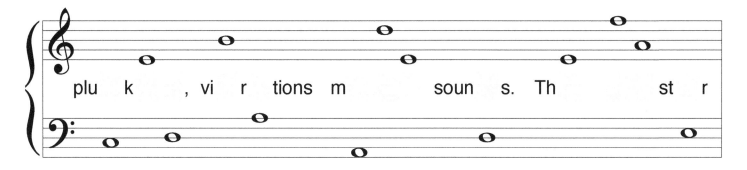

plu k , vi r tions m soun s. Th st r

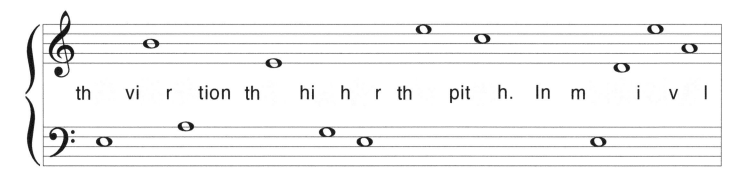

th vi r tion th hi h r th pit h. In m i v l

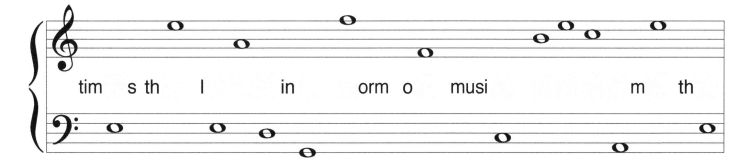

tim s th l in orm o musi m th

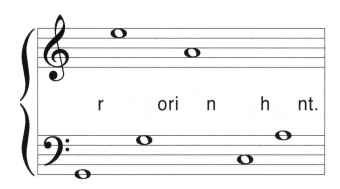

r ori n h nt.

HALF STEPS AND WHOLE STEPS
Life in the Middle Ages

In the gray boxes name the notes. Follow the direction of the arrows and draw a note to the right that is a **half step** above or below the given note. Use sharps and flats as needed.

Follow the direction of the arrows and draw a note that is a **whole step** above or below the given note. Use sharps and flats as needed.

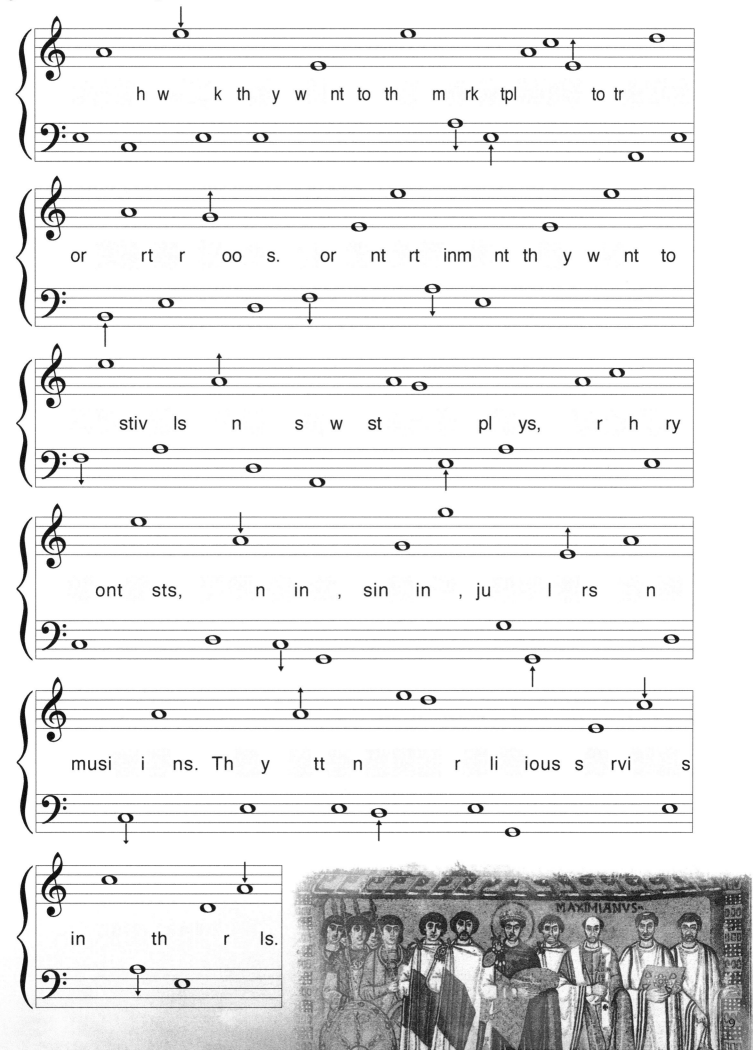

ENHARMONIC NOTES
Life in Medieval Times

1. In the gray boxes name the notes.

2. For each note in a box, draw a note that is enharmonic to that note.
    The first one is done.

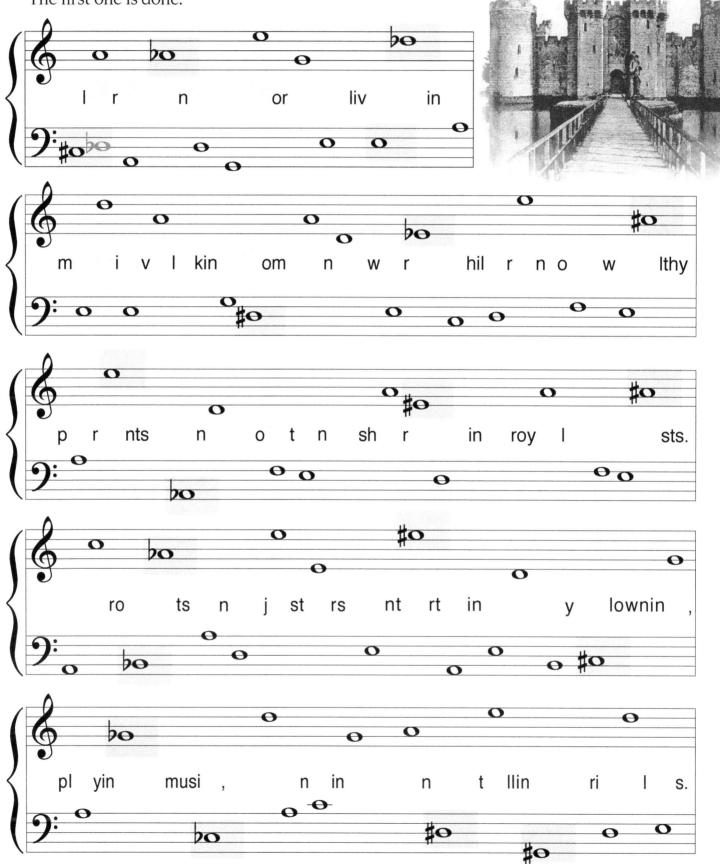

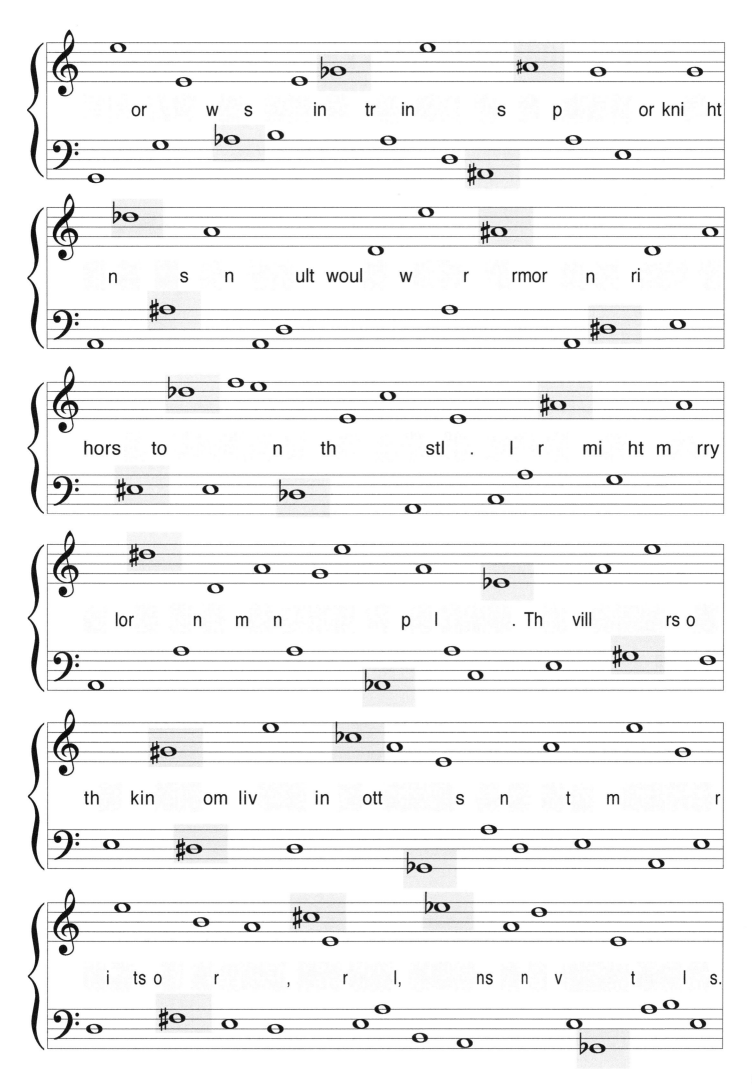

KEY OF G MAJOR – NOTES FROM LOW C TO HIGH C

Children of Renaissance Nobility

In the gray boxes name the notes. On the staff draw a sharp sign before each "F."

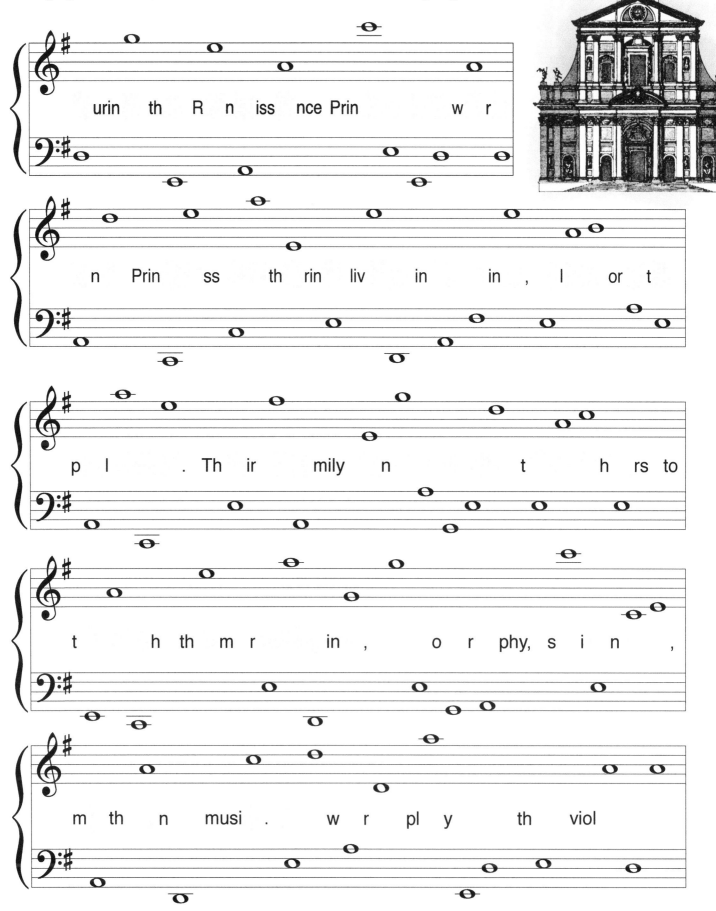

urin th R n iss nce Prin w r

n Prin ss th rin liv in in , l or t

p l . Th ir mily n t h rs to

t h th m r in , o r phy, s i n ,

m th n musi . w r pl y th viol

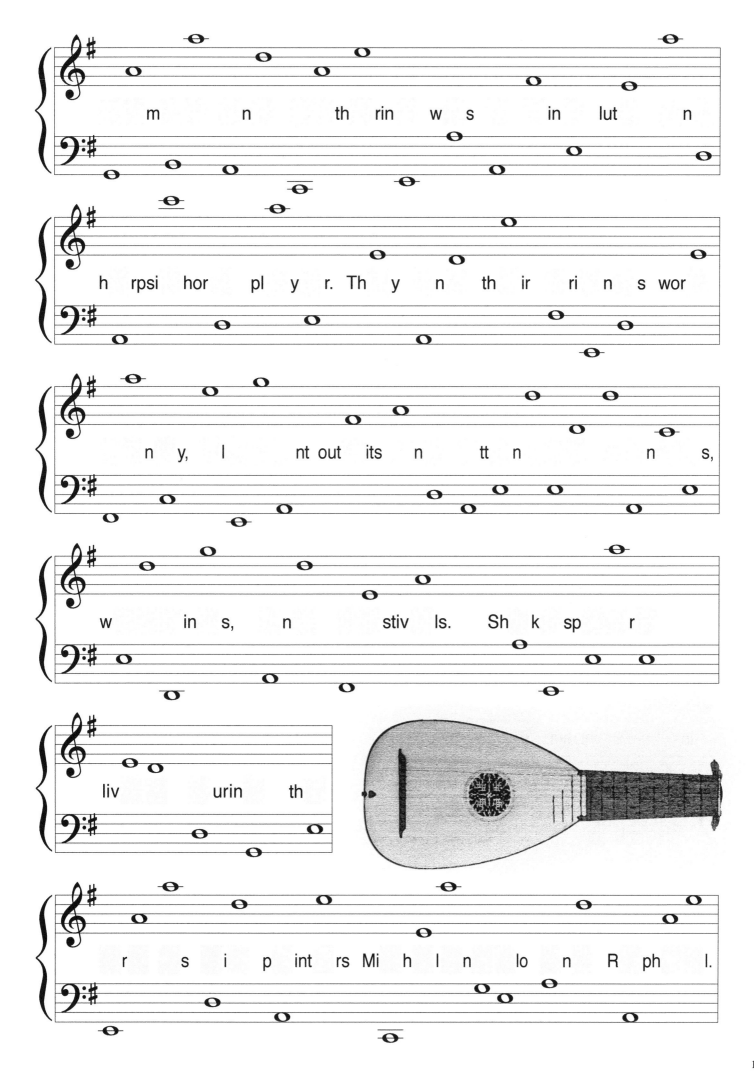

KEY OF F MAJOR

Musical Instruments Through the Ages

In the gray boxes name the notes. On the staff draw a flat sign before each "B."

pip s, h rps, n r or rs w r irst pl y

urin m i v l tim s.

pip s m rom th Mi l st.

In n i nt tim s lut s w r rv rom rs' l s.

Th or n w s irst r t n

m in l x n ri , ypt.

14

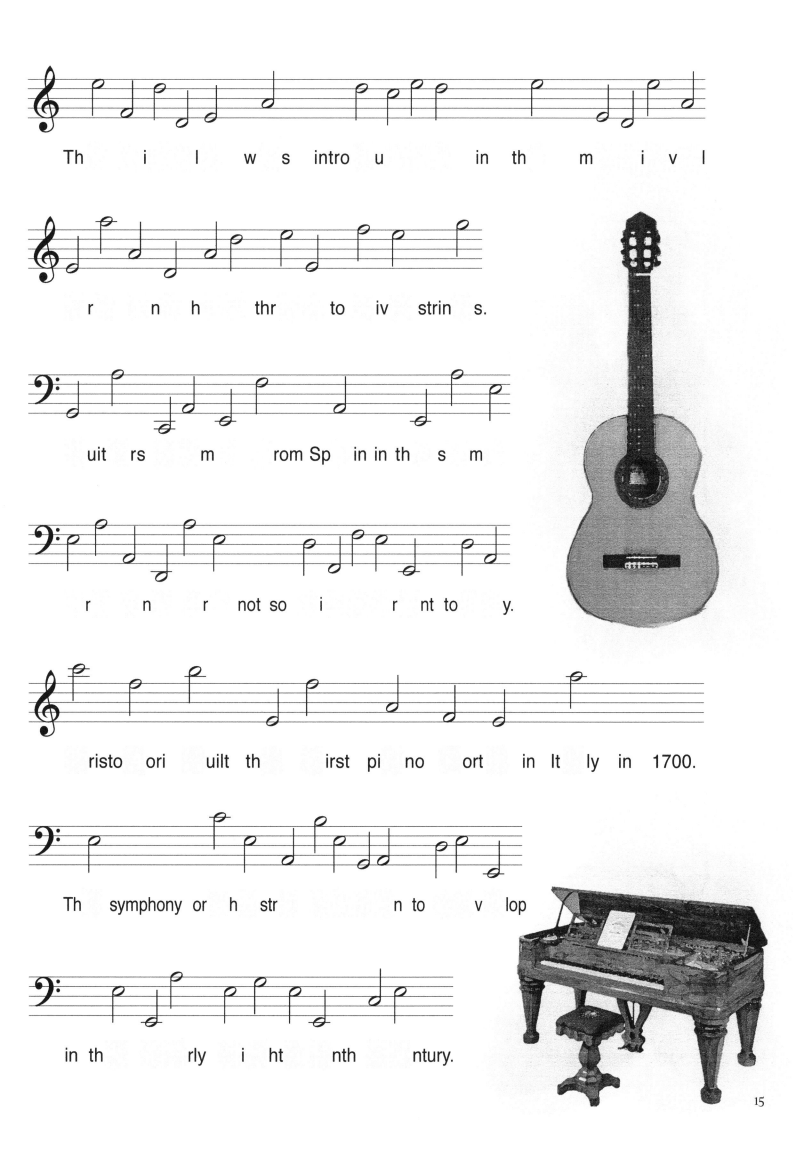

Th i l w s intro u in th m i v l

r n h thr to iv strin s.

uit rs m rom Sp in in th s m

r n r not so i r nt to y.

risto ori uilt th irst pi no ort in It ly in 1700.

Th symphony or h str n to v lop

in th rly i ht nth ntury.

KEY OF D MAJOR

The Baroque Period – A Day in the Life of J.S. Bach

In the gray boxes write the names of the notes. On the staff draw sharps before notes "F" and "C."

loth s n uil in s m n i r,

mor or tiv n l or t .

u i n s or r t op r s,

b ll ts, st ts, n hur h musi . Th h rpsi hor

w s th hi k y o r instrum nt.

KEY OF B♭ MAJOR
The Classical Period

In the gray boxes write the names of the notes. On the staff draw flats before notes "B" and "E."

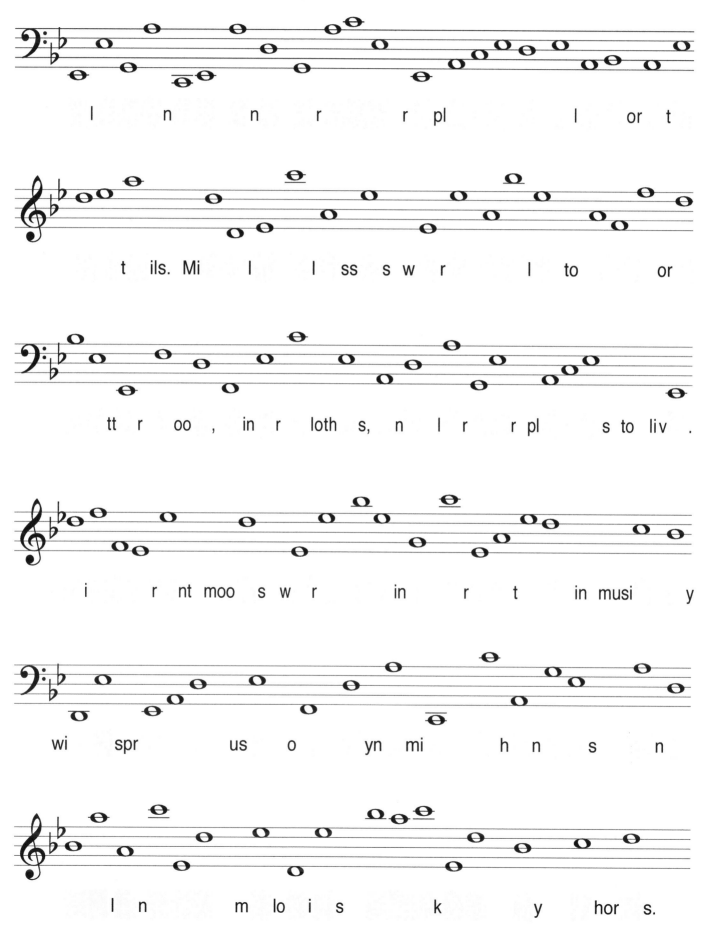

A Day in the Life of Mozart

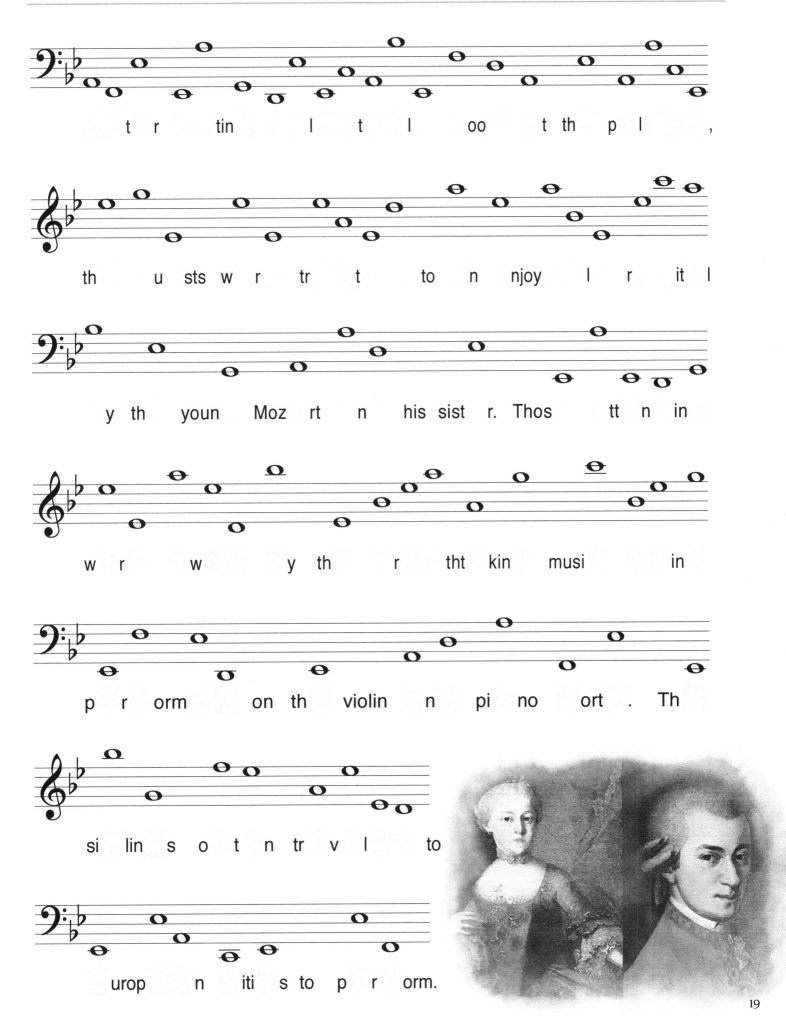

t r tin l t l oo t th p l ,

th u sts w r tr t to n njoy l r it l

y th youn Moz rt n his sist r. Thos tt n in

w r w y th r tht kin musi in

p r orm on th violin n pi no ort . Th

si lin s o t n tr v l to

urop n iti s to p r orm.

KEY OF A MAJOR
The Romantic Period

In the gray boxes write the names of the notes. Draw sharps before notes "F," "C," and "G."

A Day in the Life of Fréderic Chopin

L   i   s   n   ntl m   n o   P   ris,   r   n   , w   r

x   it   us   th   y w   r   out to h   r

r   it l   iv   n   y   th   l   im   Mr.   hopin.

Most   h   h   r   his   in   r   i   l   tu   s,

n   s   n   oth   r pi   no pi   s. Now th   y   w   r

oin   to h   r th   m   st   r hims l   . Th   y

r   t   him with   ppl   us   .

KEY OF E♭ MAJOR
The Contemporary Period

In the gray boxes write the names of the notes. On the staff draw flats before notes "B," "E," and "A."

str   t   rt   n   iz   rr   musi   m   r

urin   this   r   n   m   wi   spr   .

M   ny   i   not   pt   th   i   r   nt

pr   ti   s   n   r   ll   .   This   r   in   lu

th   Sp   n   m   ny   s   i   nti   i

is   ov   ri   s.

A Day in the Life of Igor Stravinsky

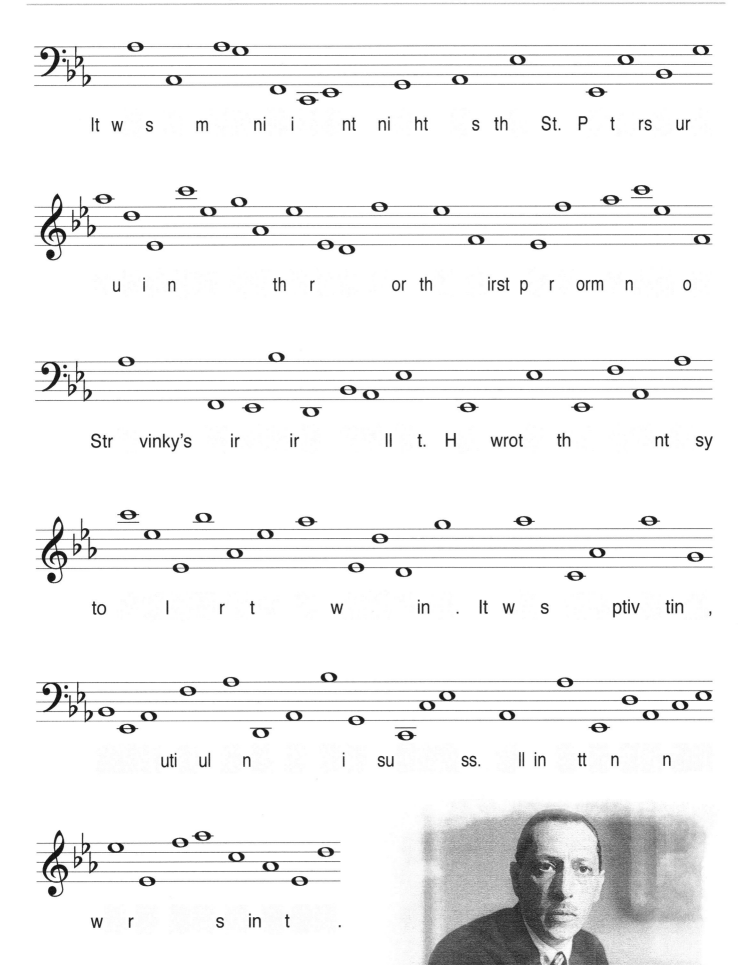

lt w s m ni i nt ni ht s th St. P t rs ur

u i n th r or th irst p r orm n o

Str vinky's ir ir ll t. H wrot th nt sy

to l r t w in . lt w s ptiv tin ,

uti ul n i su ss. ll in tt n n

w r s in t .

INTERVALS
Interesting Facts

In the gray boxes name the notes. Identify all circled intervals. The first one is done for you.

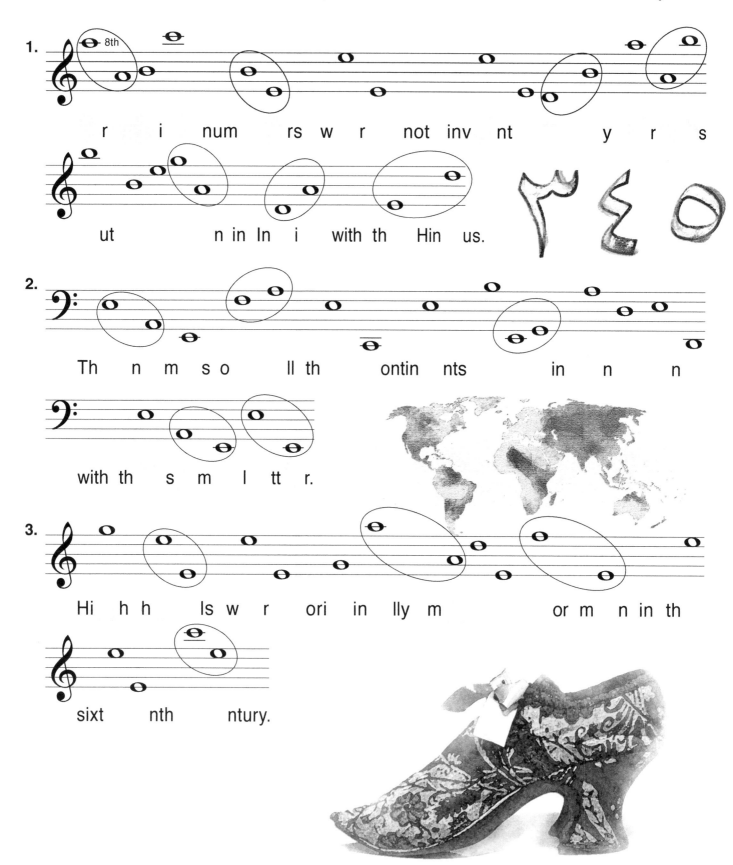

1.

r   i   num   rs w   r   not inv   nt   y   r   s

ut   n in In i   with th   Hin us.

2.

Th   n   m   s o   ll th   ontin nts   in   n   n

with th   s m   l   tt   r.

3.

Hi   h h   ls w   r   ori in lly m   or m   n in th

sixt   nth   ntury.

4. Th worl 's popul h s n rly ou l in th l st i ty y rs.

5. In 1537 n l n 's Kin H nry VII o i i lly l r ru ry 14th s St. V l ntin 's y.

6. Th l r st o th r t Pyr mi s o iz is th ol st o th S v n Won rs o th n i nt Worl .

7. Pil rims i not t pot to s us th y w r ri th y oul t l.

LEDGER LINE NOTES ABOVE THE TREBLE STAFF AND BELOW THE BASS STAFF

Music Genres

In the gray boxes name the notes to identify each music genre.

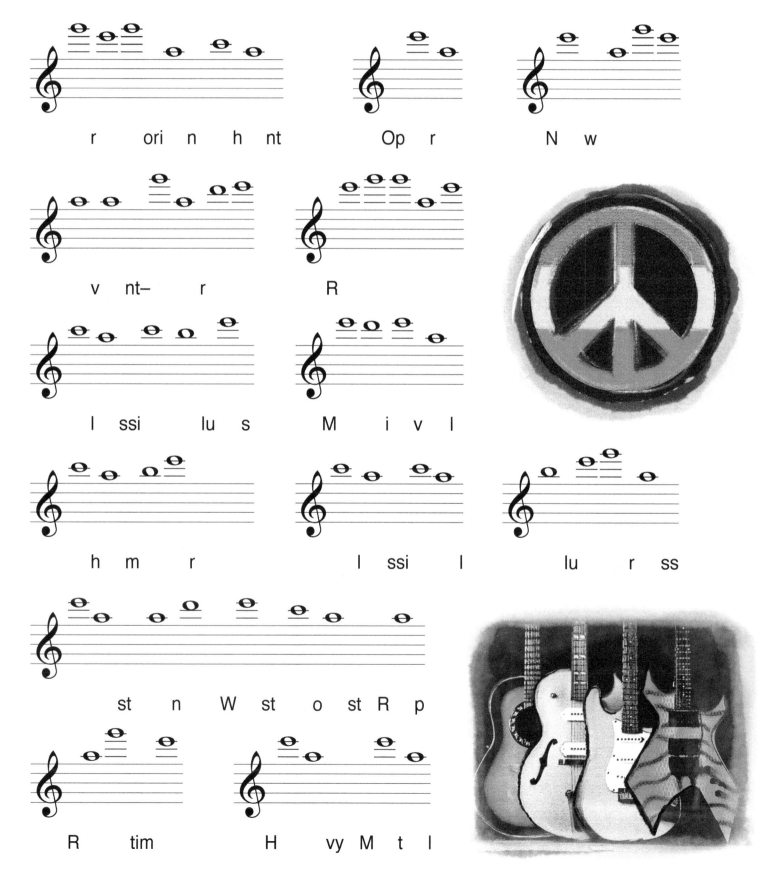

r   ori   n   h   nt

Op   r

N   w

v   nt–   r

R

l   ssi   lu   s

M   i   v   l

h   m   r

l   ssi   l

lu   r   ss

st   n   W   st   o   st   R   p

R   tim

H   vy   M   t   l

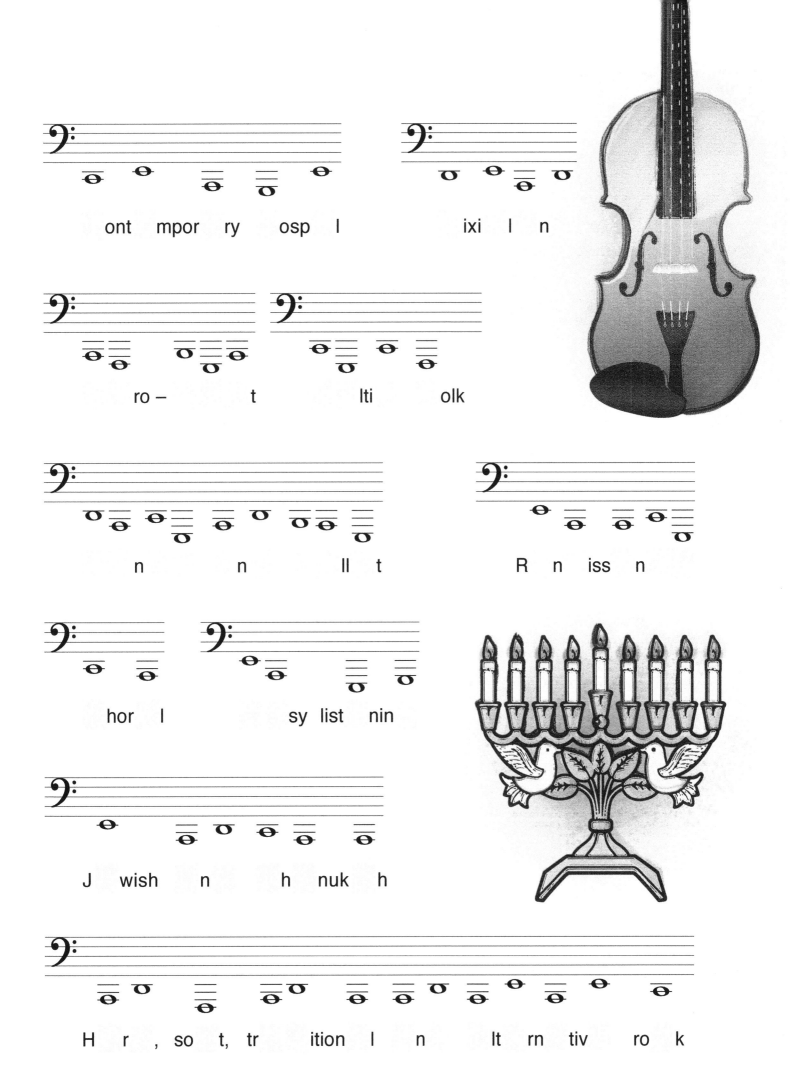

ont mpor ry   osp l   ixi l n

ro –   t   lti   olk

n   n   ll t   R   n   iss   n

hor   l   sy list nin

J   wish   n   h   nuk   h

H r , so t, tr   ition l n   lt rn tiv   ro   k

LEDGER LINE NOTES BETWEEN THE BASS AND TREBLE STAFFS

Inventions

In the gray boxes name the notes.

ut   n   r   i   l   Print   – 1455

irst   r   u   l   y   solin   –1886

Worl   wi   w   l   un   h   – 1992

irst   ontin   nt   l   r   ilro   –1869

l   tri   t   l   r   ph – 1838   R   r   r   t   – 1935

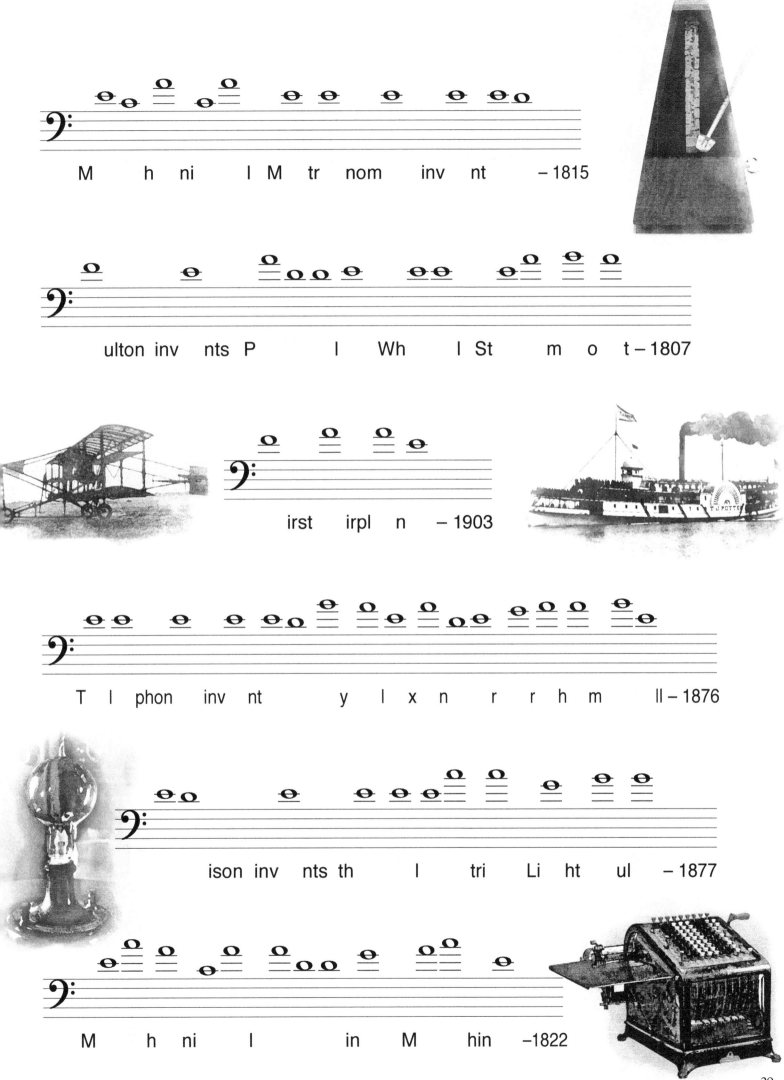

M_ _h_ni_ l M_tr_nom_ inv_nt_ _ – 1815

_ulton inv_nts P_ _l_ Wh_ l St_ m_ o_ t – 1807

_irst _irpl_n_ – 1903

T_ l_ phon_ inv_nt_ _ _y _l_x_n_ r_ r_h_m _ll – 1876

_ison inv_nts th_ _l_ _tri_ Li_ht _ul_ – 1877

M_ h_ni_ l_ _ in M_ _hin_ –1822

Important Events

In the gray boxes name the notes.

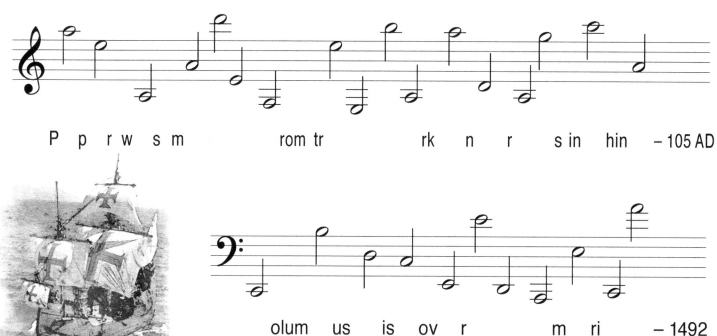

P p r w s m   rom tr   rk   n   r   s in   hin   – 105 AD

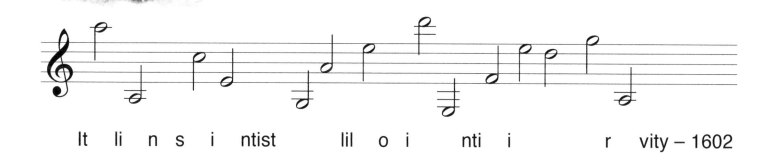

olum   us   is   ov   r   m   ri   – 1492

It   li   n   s   i   ntist   lil   o   i   nti   i   r   vity – 1602

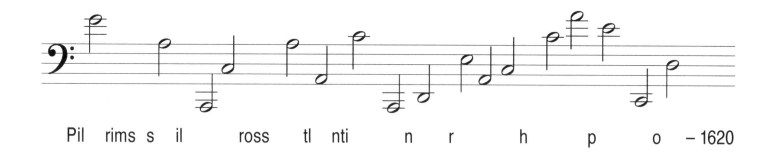

Pil   rims s   il   ross   tl nti   n   r   h   p   o – 1620

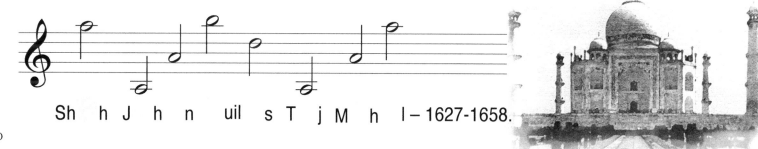

Sh   h J h   n   uil   s T   j M   h   l – 1627-1658.

l r tion o In p n n si n — 1776

r n uil s Su z n l, lo t in ypt — 1869

R io w v s i nti i y rm n s i ntist H rtz — 1887

irst sp s t llit l un h in 1957 by the Soviet Union

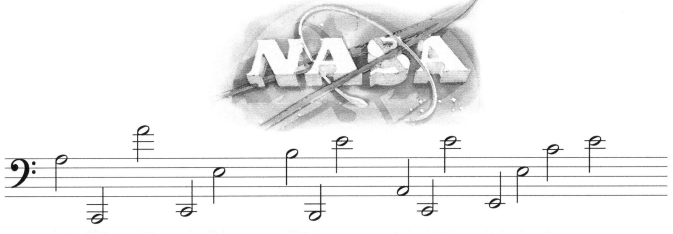

N S l un h s Hu l Sp t l s op — 1990.

NOTES ON STAFFS AND LEDGER LINES
Predictions for the Future

In the gray boxes name the notes.

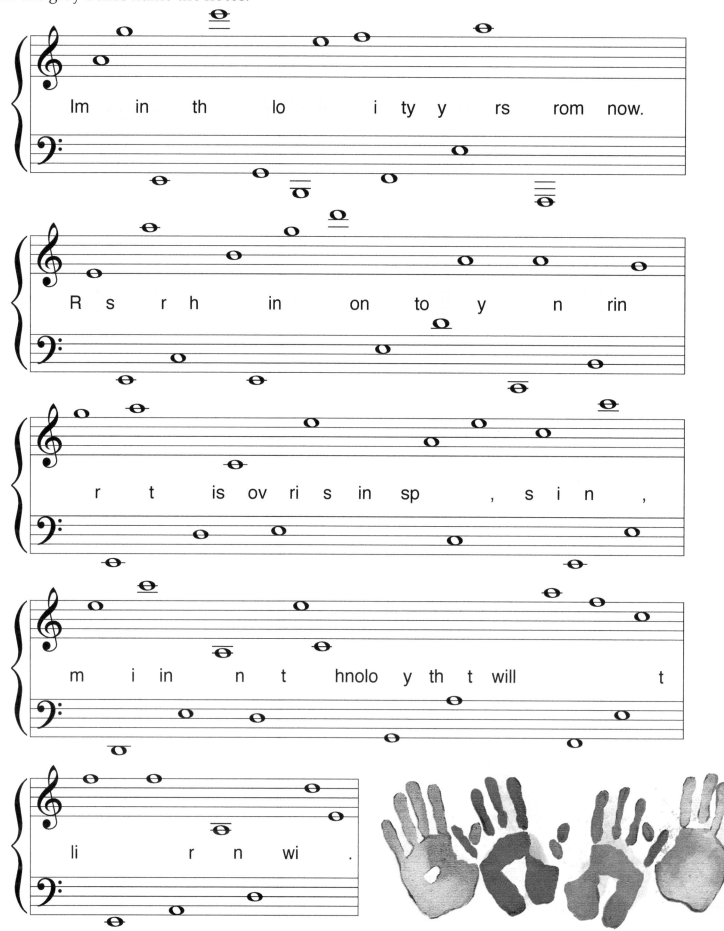

Im ___ in ___ th ___ lo ___ i ___ ty ___ y ___ rs ___ rom ___ now.

R ___ s ___ r ___ h ___ in ___ on ___ to ___ y ___ n ___ rin

r ___ t ___ is ___ ov ___ ri ___ s ___ in ___ sp ___ , ___ s ___ in ___ ,

m ___ i ___ in ___ n ___ t ___ hnolo ___ y ___ th ___ t ___ will ___ t

li ___ r ___ n ___ wi ___ .